THE CHALLENGER EXPLOSION

by Roberta Baxter

Content Consultant
Mike D. Reynolds, PhD
Dean of Liberal Arts and Sciences
Florida State College at Jacksonville

CORE LIBRARY

Published by ABDO Publishing Company, PO Box 398166, Minneapolis, MN 55439. Copyright © 2014 by Abdo Consulting Group, Inc. International copyrights reserved in all countries. No part of this book may be reproduced in any form without written permission from the publisher. The Core Library™ is a trademark and logo of ABDO Publishing Company.

Printed in the United States of America,
North Mankato, Minnesota
042013
092013

Editor: Blythe Hurley
Series Designer: Becky Daum

Library of Congress Control Number: 2013931966

Cataloging-in-Publication Data
Baxter, Roberta.
  The challenger explosion / Roberta Baxter.
   p. cm. -- (History's greatest disasters)
ISBN 978-1-61783-954-2 (lib. bdg.)
ISBN 978-1-62403-019-2 (pbk.)
Includes bibliographical references and index.
1. Challenger (Spacecraft)--Accidents--Juvenile literature. 2. Space shuttles--Accidents--Juvenile literature. 3. Space vehicle accidents--United States--Juvenile literature. I. Title.
363.12--dc23
                                                2013931966

Photo Credits: Bruce Weaver/AP Images, cover, 1, 31, 45; Bettmann/ Corbis/AP Images, 4, 32, 34; AP Images, 8; John W. Young/Bettmann/ Corbis/AP Images, 10; John Raoux/AP Images, 13; Shutterstock Images/ Red Line Editorial, Inc., 14; NASA TV/AP Images, 15, 17, 20; Smiley N. Pool/Houston Chronicle/AP Images, 18; NASA via The Columbian/AP Images, 21; NASA/AP Images, 23; Thom Baur/AP Images, 26; Red Line Editorial, Inc., 29; Pool/AP Images, 36; Bruce Schwartzman/AP Images, 38

CONTENTS

CHAPTER ONE
Space Exploration 4

CHAPTER TWO
The Space Shuttle Program . . . 10

CHAPTER THREE
Getting Ready to Fly 18

CHAPTER FOUR
Liftoff and Disaster 26

CHAPTER FIVE
After the Disaster 34

Important Dates .42

Stop and Think .44

Glossary 46

Learn More 47

Index 48

About the Author 48

SPACE EXPLORATION

On Tuesday, January 28, 1986, seven astronauts in blue jumpsuits boarded the space shuttle *Challenger*. The countdown began. The engines started with a roar of fire and smoke. *Challenger*'s flight had begun.

In 1986 the space shuttle program had been running for five years. In that time, *Challenger* had been part of many firsts. It had taken the first US

Ready to launch into space, *Challenger*'s crew heads for the launchpad.

woman, the first African American, and the first Canadian into space. It was also the first shuttle to complete a night launch and a night landing. This was to be *Challenger*'s tenth flight. It was the space shuttle program's twenty-fourth flight overall.

A private citizen would be a part of the crew for the first time on this mission. Teacher Christa McAuliffe planned to teach two lessons from *Challenger*. On launch day, students came to the John F. Kennedy Space Center in Florida to watch the launch. Thousands more watched on televisions in their classrooms.

The History of Manned Spaceflight

By the mid-1900s, people had dreamed of going into space for centuries. In 1958 the US government created the National Aeronautics and Space Administration (NASA). This agency would oversee US spaceflight. In 1961 a man from the Soviet Union became the first human to travel into space.

Spaceflight is dangerous. There is no oxygen and a feeling of weightlessness. In the early years of space travel, astronauts traveled in pods on top of rockets filled with explosive fuels.

In 1962 astronaut John Glenn became the first American to orbit Earth. During this mission there was concern that the heat shield on his spaceship might have come loose. The heat shield is the part of the ship that protects it from the extreme heat that occurs when the craft returns to Earth. Glenn returned safely. NASA later found that the problem was caused by a broken instrument.

Yuri Gargarin and the Soviet Union Space Program

Russian astronauts are called cosmonauts. The first person to experience spaceflight was a cosmonaut named Yuri Gagarin. He flew his mission on April 12, 1961. His spacecraft was part of a series of missions known as the Vostok program. This program completed six manned spaceflights from 1961 to 1963.

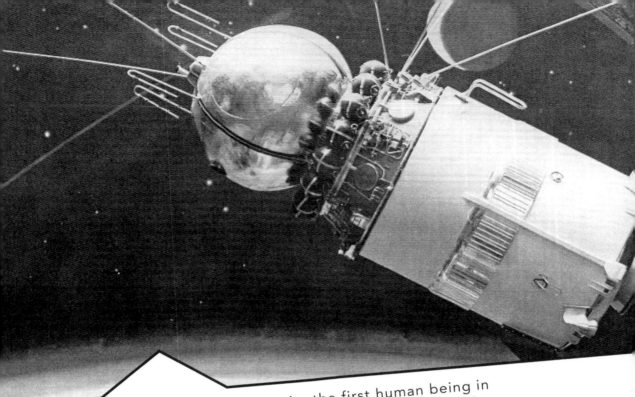

Cosmonaut Yuri Gargarin, the first human being in space, orbited Earth in a spaceship similar to this Vostok-type vehicle.

On January 27, 1967, three US astronauts were testing *Apollo 1* while it was still on the launchpad. A fire inside the capsule, or spaceship, killed the astronauts. After this accident, NASA made capsules more fire resistant.

The Soviet Union also had a disaster in 1967. One of their spacecraft crashed during its return to Earth, killing its one crew member. And in 1970 *Apollo 13* had an emergency in space when one of the ship's oxygen tanks exploded. It almost didn't return to Earth.

Challenger was checked carefully by NASA scientists to ensure that it was ready to go into space. The ship's crew believed they were stepping into the record books by having the first private citizen on a space shuttle flight. Instead people would remember them because of what happened 73 seconds into their flight.

CHAPTER TWO

THE SPACE SHUTTLE PROGRAM

In 1969 Americans Neil Armstrong and Buzz Aldrin became the first humans to land on the moon. The next step into space was building a space station. But some of the loads these missions would need to carry would be too big for the rockets NASA's spaceships used to escape Earth's gravity. NASA also wanted to make space travel less expensive. NASA needed a spacecraft that was cheaper to operate and

Challenger heads into space for its second mission.

could carry heavy loads. The space shuttle program was the answer.

The Space Shuttle Program Is Born

Scientists and engineers designed the space shuttle to be about the size of a large airplane. Three main engines launched the shuttle into space. More power came from two rocket boosters full of fuel.

When the shuttle lifted off, these solid rocket boosters, called SRBs, and the main engines all burned fuel. After two minutes, the SRBs used up their fuel and were released. Parachutes opened up on the noses of the SRBs. The parachutes allowed them to fall gently into

The Space Shuttle's First Flight

The space shuttle *Columbia* launched for its first spaceflight on April 12, 1981. Two astronauts, commander John Young and pilot Robert Crippen, were on board. Their mission was to test the shuttle's systems in space. They flew for two days and then landed safely at Edwards Air Force Base in California. All of the shuttle's systems worked well.

The space shuttles used large external fuel tanks to supply them with enough fuel to overcome Earth's gravity.

the ocean. A ship then picked them up. NASA would reuse the SRBs on other shuttle missions.

Liquid fuel for the shuttle engines was stored in a large external tank attached to the shuttle. Once the shuttle launched and burned that fuel, it released the external tank. The tank burned up as it fell into the atmosphere.

Smaller engines provided the power for the shuttle to stay in orbit. These smaller engines also

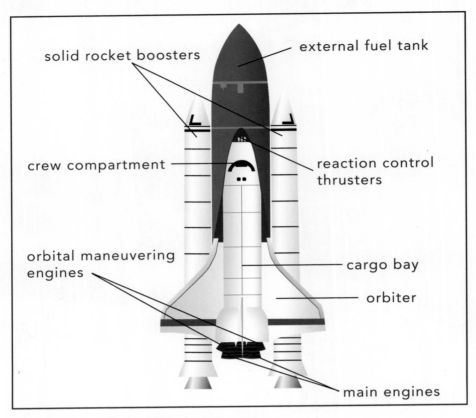

solid rocket boosters

external fuel tank

crew compartment

reaction control thrusters

orbital maneuvering engines

cargo bay

orbiter

main engines

The Parts of the Space Shuttle

The shuttle's system had several parts. After reading about the shuttle, what did you imagine it looked like? How has that idea changed after looking at this diagram?

allowed the shuttle to return to Earth. Instead of landing in the ocean, the shuttle glided to a landing on a runway like an airplane.

A cargo bay took up most of the space in the shuttle. The cargo bay could hold pieces of the space station or satellites that would be launched into orbit.

Space shuttle *Discovery*'s robot arm takes a picture of the docking port in its cargo bay.

The shuttle also had a robot arm. This arm could lift large equipment in and out of the cargo bay. It could also release satellites into space. Some missions also had a portable lab in the cargo bay. The astronauts were able to perform science experiments in space inside this lab.

Once a mission was over, the shuttle returned to Earth. Special tiles on the bottom of the shuttle protected it from the heat that builds up when objects enter the atmosphere.

NASA used the shuttle and its SRBs many times. From 1981 to 2011, shuttles launched and returned several times a year. The year 1986 was supposed to be the busiest year ever for the shuttles.

Altogether, NASA built six shuttles. But one of them, *Enterprise*, never flew in space. NASA used it only for tests to make

The Teacher in Space Program

On August 27, 1984, President Ronald Reagan announced the Teacher in Space program. NASA wanted to send a teacher into space. The teacher would communicate with students while in orbit. Teachers who wanted to be a part of the program answered many questions. They underwent medical tests and interviews. NASA chose Christa McAuliffe out of thousands of applicants. She was a high school social studies and history teacher from Concord, New Hampshire. McAuliffe called her flight the ultimate field trip.

Astronauts Michael Foale, right, and Bernard Harris Jr., left, are tethered to Discovery's robot arm during a space walk.

sure the shuttles could land correctly. Five shuttles flew in space. They were *Columbia*, *Challenger*, *Discovery*, *Atlantis*, and *Endeavor*. Together they flew more than 513 million miles (826 million km).

CHAPTER THREE

GETTING READY TO FLY

Like all astronauts, *Challenger*'s crew trained and studied for months for each shuttle mission. They tested themselves to make sure they knew how to operate all of the shuttle's equipment in space. They also had to be in excellent physical condition. They exercised every day.

The crew of one of Atlantis's missions practices docking with the International Space Station using model equipment.

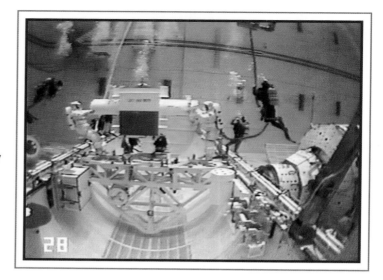

Astronauts Jerry Ross and James Newman practice working under water, which is very similar to working in space.

Training for Work in Outer Space

Astronauts practiced inside a model shuttle. The model shuttle had all the same equipment as the real shuttle. Astronauts practiced handling emergencies and using the robot arm. If they would be doing experiments in space, they practiced those on the ground too.

Some of the astronauts' training took place under water. Working under water is very similar to working in space.

More training took place on an airplane nicknamed the Vomit Comet. This is an air force plane

The crew of one of Atlantis's missions trains for zero-gravity conditions.

called a KC-135. The astronauts rode in the back of the plane. The back had no seats. It was just an open space. The pilot flew the plane up into the sky. Then, curving back toward Earth, the pilot plunged the plane down. For the astronauts, this created the feeling of being in outer space with no gravity. The crew was able to float and bounce inside the plane. Some astronauts felt as if they might vomit during this training.

Challenger's Crew

Challenger had a seven-person crew. Commander Francis "Dick" Scobee had flown on two previous shuttle flights. Pilot Michael Smith was a former navy pilot. He had been an astronaut for five years. Mission Specialists Judith Resnik, Ellison Onizuka, and Ronald McNair had all flown on one shuttle flight before. For Payload Specialist Gregory Jarvis, *Challenger* would be the first shuttle flight. The last member of the crew was Christa McAuliffe. She was a social studies and history teacher.

Challenger Waits for Columbia's Return

NASA scheduled *Challenger*'s flight for January 23, 1986. But the launch was delayed because of problems with another shuttle, *Columbia*. *Challenger* needed some of the parts on *Columbia*. Also, NASA did not want to have two shuttles in space at the same time. So *Challenger* had to wait for *Columbia* to return from space.

Columbia had gone into space later than planned. Then rain delayed its landing back on Earth. Finally *Columbia* landed on January 18. But it landed

Challenger's crew. Back row, from left: Ellison Onizuka, Christa McAuliffe, Gregory Jarvis, and Judith Resnik. Front row, from left: Michael Smith, Francis "Dick" Scobee, and Ronald McNair.

in California, not Florida. NASA took the parts needed for *Challenger* off *Columbia* and flew them to Florida. NASA scheduled *Challenger* for launch on January 25.

More Delays

When NASA delays a launch, astronauts say that it has been scrubbed. NASA scrubbed the January

25 launch because of bad weather. The launch was put off until January 26. Then NASA delayed the launch again. Finally, on January 27, *Challenger's* crew prepared for liftoff. Launchpad workers closed the door of the shuttle. But one of the switches indicated that the door was not closed properly. The workers and the astronauts eventually figured out a way to make sure the door was closed. But this took a long time. NASA scrubbed the launch again. It scheduled *Challenger* to fly the next day, Tuesday, January 28.

Delays and Scrubs

Challenger was supposed to be the first space shuttle to launch during 1986. But *Columbia* actually took over that position. This was because NASA had to delay *Columbia's* mission seven times. This was a record number of delays that affected launches for both *Challenger* and *Columbia*. Finally on January 12, 1986, *Columbia* launched. Tired NASA crews could finally prepare for *Challenger's* launch.

EXPLORE ONLINE

Chapter Three talks about how astronauts train for working in space. The Web site below focuses on the same subject. As you know, every source is different. How is the information given in this Web site different from the information in this chapter? What information is the same? How do the sources present information differently? What can you learn from this Web site? Write a few sentences exploring these questions. Be sure to include details that support your ideas.

Astronaut Training
www.mycorelibrary.com/challenger

CHAPTER FOUR

LIFTOFF AND DISASTER

On January 27 NASA prepared to launch *Challenger*. First several groups of people had to report that their systems were go, or ready. Preparing for a spaceflight takes time and careful attention.

All seemed to be going as planned as Challenger lifted off on January 28, 1986.

Preparing for Liftoff

Launching a space shuttle was no simple task. NASA had to check many different systems before it could declare the shuttle ready. This process was known as the launch status check, or the go/no go poll. The NASA test director, or NTD, was the leader of the shuttle test team. The NTD was responsible for ensuring that the shuttle's crew and all its systems were ready for liftoff. The NTD reported to the launch director. *Challenger*'s launch director was responsible for declaring the mission ready for launch.

Cold Weather Again Threatens the Launch

The weather turned cold on the evening of January 27. The rocket engineers who had designed *Challenger*'s SRBs were worried about the temperature. The shuttle's rockets were built in sections full of solid fuel. Rubber rings called O-rings sealed the joints between these sections. Rubber becomes stiffer when it gets cold. If these rings failed, they might leak hot gas from burning fuel during liftoff. The shuttle's engineers recommended that the shuttle not launch if it was colder than

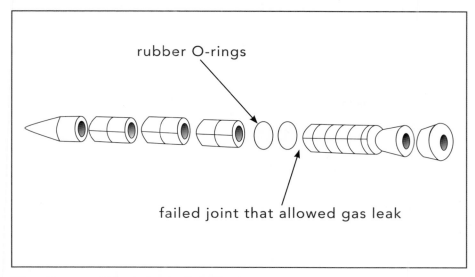

rubber O-rings

failed joint that allowed gas leak

The Space Shuttle's O-Rings

This diagram shows the shuttle's rubber O-rings, which engineers feared would become stiff due to cold weather on the day of the launch. This could cause burning gas to leak from an SRB. Compare the way in which this information is shown visually with how the same information is presented in this book. How are the diagram and the book similar? How are they different?

53 degrees Fahrenheit (12°C). The temperature that day was only about 29 degrees Fahrenheit (1.7°C). But NASA officials did not think the cold would be a problem as long as there was no ice on the shuttle by launch time.

Icicles hung from the shuttle on the morning of January 28. But the ice began to melt once the sun came up. At 11:38 a.m., the engines fired. The shuttle rose slowly from the launchpad.

A Tragic Malfunction

Challenger rose through a clear blue sky, leaving a stream of smoke. At 73 seconds into the flight, observers saw a large puff of white smoke. Two lines of white smoke twisted away from that big cloud. Many thought that this was a normal part of the launch procedure.

These observers were wrong. The two lines of smoke were the SRBs speeding away from the broken shuttle. *Challenger* had blown up, killing the crew inside. Pieces of the shuttle and the external tank fell into the ocean. No one who saw the picture of those smoke trails ever forgot it and what it meant.

As *Challenger* fell from the sky, the reactions of those watching were immediate. The crowds of family and friends who had come to watch the launch were stunned and heartbroken. So were those watching on television around the world.

Challenger explodes shortly after taking off from the Kennedy Space Center.

In a speech later that day, President Ronald Reagan expressed the feelings of many who were grieving. He shared his own sadness about the disaster. He also reassured Americans that the space program would continue despite the tragedy.

Americans mourned the deaths of *Challenger*'s seven crew members. But many people still believed that the space program was important to the country.

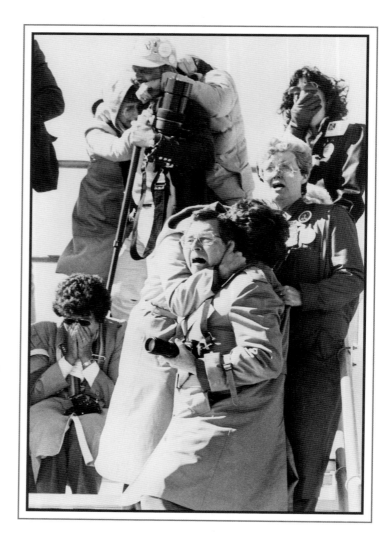

Spectators react in horror as *Challenger* explodes shortly after liftoff.

Most Americans believed the benefits of the program were worth its costs, even when that sometimes meant the loss of human lives. Americans were eager for the space shuttles to fly again. But this would take some time.

Roger Boisjoly was an engineer for the maker of *Challenger's* solid rocket motors. In a memo written on July 31, 1985, Boisjoly and another engineer recommended delaying all shuttle launches during cold weather. They had evidence of O-ring problems on previous flights:

> *This letter is written to insure that management is fully aware of the seriousness of the current O-ring erosion problem in the SRM [solid rocket motor] joints from an engineering standpoint. . . . The result would be a catastrophe of the highest order—loss of human life. . . . It is my honest and very real fear that if we do not take immediate action to dedicate a team to solve the problem with the field joint having the number one priority, then we stand in jeopardy of losing a flight along with all the launch pad facilities.*

Source: Diane Vaughan. The Challenger Launch Decision. Chicago: The University of Chicago Press, 1996. Print. 447–48.

Consider Your Audience

Read Boisjoly's memo closely. How could you adapt it for a different audience, such as your parents or younger friends? Write a blog post conveying this same information for the new audience. What is the best way to get your point across to this audience?

CHAPTER FIVE

AFTER THE DISASTER

After the *Challenger* explosion, NASA studied the cause of the accident. President Reagan thought that a group that was not part of NASA should also investigate. He appointed a presidential commission to collect evidence and learn what had happened. This commission included astronaut Neil Armstrong, the first man to walk on the moon. Sally Ride, the first US woman in space, was also a member.

US Navy personnel lift large pieces of debris from *Challenger* out of the ocean near Cape Canaveral, Florida.

Members of President Reagan's commission walk past solid rocket boosters and an external shuttle tank at the John F. Kennedy Space Center.

So was Chuck Yeager, the first man to fly faster than the speed of sound.

The commission talked to people from NASA and the companies that made the shuttle's parts. It also questioned those who had examined the pieces of the shuttle pulled out of the ocean. The commission reported that the cause of the explosion was the O-rings on one of the SRBs. The cold had indeed made the rubber stiffer. This allowed hot gases to escape from the SRB. A flame came out of one loose joint. This caused the SRB to hit the external tank full of explosive fuel. The tank exploded, tearing the shuttle apart.

Moving Forward

The tragic explosion of *Challenger* didn't end US space travel. NASA used what it had learned from the disaster to make its other shuttles safer. Two and a half years after the *Challenger* explosion, NASA was ready to launch another shuttle.

On September 29, 1988, the shuttle *Discovery* was launched. It spent four days in space before landing safely in California. NASA was back in business.

The *Columbia* Disaster

The space shuttles would fly many more missions after the *Challenger* disaster. But these later missions were not without accidents.

In 1981 *Columbia* had been the first shuttle to fly in space. On January 16, 2003, a seven-person crew blasted off for a research mission on *Columbia*.

Space shuttle *Discovery* arrives at Dulles International Airport in Virginia on the back of a NASA 747 aircraft.

When the shuttle launched, a piece of foam came off the external tank. This foam hit the left wing of the shuttle. The astronauts and NASA did not know the foam had damaged the wing.

As the shuttle reentered the atmosphere on February 1, the damaged wing area let heat into the shuttle. *Columbia* came apart, killing all seven crew members. A group of experts would again study the evidence related to the disaster to learn what had happened. *Discovery* would once more be the first shuttle to return to flight after a disaster. It went into space two and a half years after the *Columbia* disaster.

The End of the Shuttle Program

NASA ended the space shuttle program in 2011. The shuttles were getting old. NASA would use the money saved by ending the program to pay for newer and better spacecraft.

The space shuttles flew 135 missions from 1981 to 2011. *Atlantis* was the last of the shuttles to fly. It reached the International Space Station to deliver parts and supplies and launch a satellite. It then landed at the John F. Kennedy Space Center in Florida.

Retired Space Shuttles

The four remaining space shuttles are now on display at museums and space centers around the country. *Enterprise* is at the Intrepid Sea, Air & Space Museum in New York. *Discovery* is at the Smithsonian National Air and Space Museum in Virginia. *Endeavor* is at the California Science Center in Los Angeles. And *Atlantis* is housed at the John F. Kennedy Space Center in Florida.

To Mars and Beyond?

NASA has plans for a new spacecraft called the Multi-Purpose Crew Vehicle, or MPCV. NASA plans to send this craft to the moon, asteroids, Mars, and the International Space Station. Each MPCV spacecraft will carry a crew of four or more astronauts.

Lost but Not Forgotten

Americans have not forgotten *Challenger*'s crew. Communities have named schools after the crew all around the country. In July 1986 the families of the crew created the Challenger Center for Space Science Education. This organization has built Challenger Learning Centers throughout the United States, as well as in Canada, the United Kingdom, and South Korea. Students can participate in pretend space missions at these centers.

Challenger's crew is also honored by a special spot on Mars. The Mars Rover *Opportunity* landed on Mars on January 25, 2004. NASA named the spot where it landed the Challenger Memorial Station.

President Ronald Reagan's speech after the *Challenger* accident talked about the importance of continued space exploration:

> *I know it is hard to understand, but sometimes painful things like this happen. It's all part of the process of exploration and discovery. It's all part of taking a chance and expanding man's horizons. The future doesn't belong to the fainthearted . . . it belongs to the brave. The Challenger crew was pulling us into the future, and we'll continue to follow them. . . .*
>
> *We will never forget them, nor the last time we saw them, this morning, as they prepared for the journey and waved good-bye and "slipped the surly bonds of earth" to "touch the face of God."*

Source: Ronald Reagan. "Speech on the Challenger Disaster." TeachingAmericanHistory.org. Ashbrook Center at Ashland University, 2006–12. Web. Accessed February 3, 2013.

Changing Minds

In this speech, President Reagan expresses his position that space exploration should continue in spite of the *Challenger* disaster. Take a position on the space program and its importance to our country. Then imagine that your best friend has the opposite opinion. Write a short essay trying to change your friend's mind. Make sure you explain your opinion and your reasons for it.

IMPORTANT DATES

1962

John Glenn becomes the first American to orbit Earth.

1967

A fire in the Apollo 1 capsule kills three US astronauts while they are running tests on the launchpad in January.

1967

The Soviet Union loses a cosmonaut when his capsule crashes during landing.

1986

Challenger is scheduled to launch on January 23, 25, 26, and 27. NASA delays these launches.

1986

Challenger explodes 73 seconds after launches on January 28.

1988

Discovery becomes the first shuttle to return to space after the *Challenger* disaster.

1970

Apollo 13 has an emergency in space and almost doesn't return to Earth.

1981

Columbia becomes the first space shuttle to launch, completing a two-day mission and returning safely.

1984

President Ronald Reagan announces the Teacher in Space program.

2003

The space shuttle *Columbia* disintegrates, killing all seven crew members as the shuttle reenters the atmosphere.

2005

Discovery once again becomes the first shuttle to return to flight after a disaster, this time after the loss of *Columbia*.

2011–2012

The shuttle fleet is retired and the remaining four shuttles are put on display around the country.

STOP AND THINK

Why Do I Care?

Many people feel that space travel has improved life on Earth. It has changed how we look at our planet. Many new inventions were developed due to the space program. Do you think space travel is important? If so, why? How has your life been changed because of the space program?

Take a Stand

Some people feel that the government should use the money we spend on the space program to feed people, build houses, or improve our health care system. What do you think? If it were your decision, would you spend tax money on the space program or not? Write a short essay explaining your opinion. Be sure to list your reasons and include facts to support them.

Say What?

This book uses vocabulary that might not be familiar to you. Find five words in this book that are new to you, and use a dictionary to find out what they mean. Write the meanings in your own words. Then write a short paragraph using the new words.

You Are There

What if you had been at *Challenger*'s last launch? Write a paragraph describing how you would have felt when the shuttle exploded. What would you have wanted to do to comfort the families and others around you? How might the tragedy have affected your views on space travel?

GLOSSARY

countdown
a backward count to the moment a spacecraft's rockets fire for a launch

external tank
a large container of fuel attached to the outside of the space shuttle

launch
the process of firing rockets to boost a spacecraft into space

mission specialist
an astronaut who performs experiments, uses the robotic arm of the shuttle, and performs other mission tasks

orbit
the curved path of a celestial object or spacecraft around a star, planet, or moon

orbiter
another name for the space shuttle

O-ring
a rubber ring used to seal the joints between the space shuttle's SRB sections

reentry
returning to Earth through the atmosphere

solid rocket booster (SRB)
a rocket full of solid fuel that is attached to a launch vehicle to provide enough power for it to launch; the space shuttles each used two SRBs

spacecraft
a vehicle for space travel, including a capsule and rocket boosters

LEARN MORE

Books

Burgess, Colin. *Animals in Space.* New York: Springer, 2007.

Nicolson, Cynthia Pratt. *Discover Space.* Toronto: Kids Can Press, 2005.

Stott, Carole. *Space Exploration.* New York: DK Publishing, 2009.

Web Links

To learn more about the *Challenger* disaster, visit ABDO Publishing Company online at **www.abdopublishing.com**. Web sites about the *Challenger* disaster are featured on our Book Links page. These links are routinely monitored and updated to provide the most current information available.

Visit **www.mycorelibrary.com** for free additional tools for teachers and students.

INDEX

Aldrin, Buzz, 11
Apollo 1, 8
Apollo 13, 8–9
Armstrong, Neil, 11, 35
Atlantis, 17, 39

Boisjoly, Roger, 33

Challenger Center
   for Space Science
   Education, 40
Challenger Learning
   Centers, 40
Challenger Memorial
   Station, 40
Columbia, 12, 17,
   22–23, 24, 37–39
Crippen, Robert, 12

Discovery, 17, 37, 38–39

Endeavor, 17, 39

Enterprise, 16–17, 39
external fuel tank, 13,
   14, 30, 36–37

Gargarin, Yuri, 7
Glenn, John, 7

International Space
   Station, 39, 40

Jarvis, Gregory, 22
John F. Kennedy Space
   Center, 6, 39

Mars, 40
Mars Rover
   Opportunity, 40
McAuliffe, Christa, 6,
   16, 22
McNair, Ronald, 22
Multi-Purpose Crew
   Vehicle (MPCV), 40

Onizuka, Ellison, 22
O-rings, 28–29, 33, 36

Reagan, Ronald, 16, 31,
   35, 41
Resnik, Judith, 22
Ride, Sally, 35–36

Scobee, Francis "Dick,"
   22
Smith, Michael, 22
solid rocket boosters
   (SRBs), 12–13, 14, 16,
   28, 29, 30, 36–37

Teacher in Space
   program, 16

Vostok program, 7

Yeager, Chuck, 36
Young, John, 12

ABOUT THE AUTHOR

Roberta Baxter has been intrigued by space travel since listening to John Glenn's flight in her classroom. Her writing has covered science, history, and biography for students of all ages. Her published work includes more than 15 books.